By Peter Parks

CONTENTS

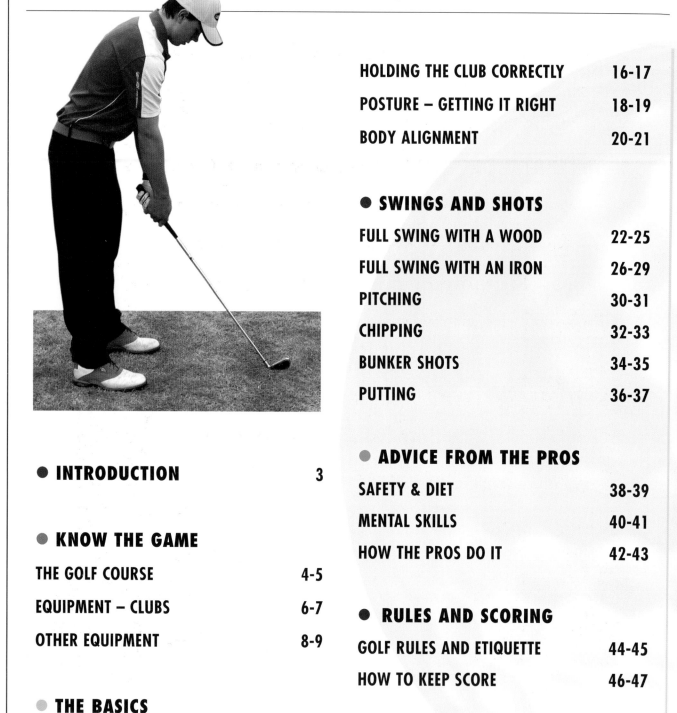

INTRODUCTION

Golf is a game that can be enjoyed by people of all ages, and is an ideal sport for anyone looking for a new challenge. It is played outside in the countryside, and since every golf course in the world is unique, each course you play is a different experience. It is a very sociable game, and a good way to make new friends. Unlike other sports, golf can be enjoyed by players of very different standards playing together – this is because of the way the scoring system works. Many celebrities enjoy playing golf in their spare time, including David Beckham, Justin Timberlake and Robbie Williams. So why not find out for yourself why golf is so much fun!

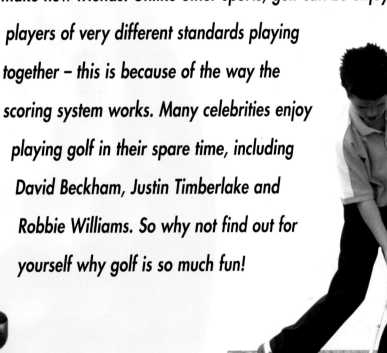

LEFT- AND RIGHT-HANDEDNESS

This book is written from the point of view of a right-handed player.
If you are left-handed, you must remember that the illustrations are a mirror image of the position you should adopt. You will have to use your right hand when the instructions say left, and vice versa.

THE GOLF COURSE

*G*olf is a game played over a course of 18 holes. Each hole measures a different length – this length will determine the par of the hole. Par is the number of shots a professional would take on an average day to complete the hole, and this gives the player a guide to how many shots it should take them based on their ability.

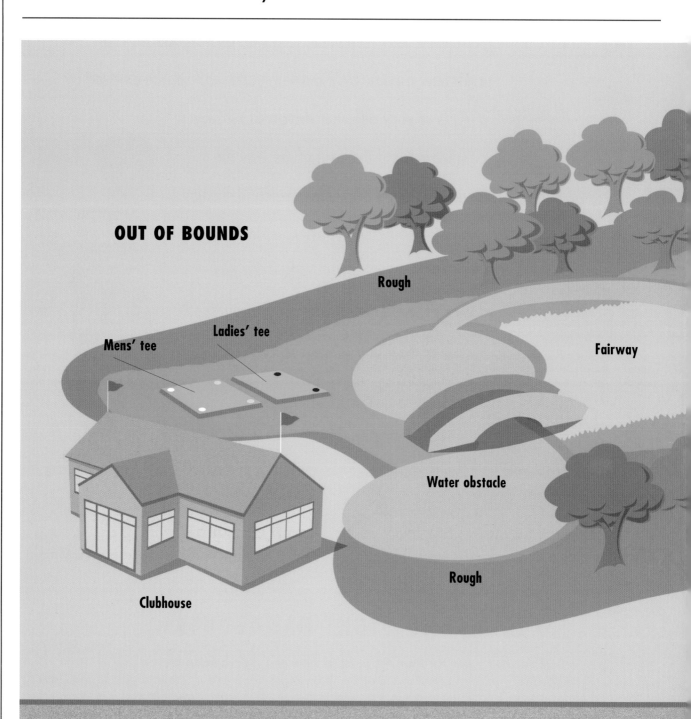

OUT OF BOUNDS

Rough

Fairway

Mens' tee

Ladies' tee

Water obstacle

Rough

Clubhouse

There are three different pars for a golf hole (depending on the length of the hole). They are par 3, par 4 or par 5. Par 3s are the shortest and par 5s are the longest.

The player must hit the ball from the teeing ground towards the green and try to avoid any of the hazards that are on the hole. The hazards can be in the form of water (ponds or streams), sand bunkers, trees or rough (long grass). Once on the green, the player must get the ball into the hole in the least amount of putts possible.

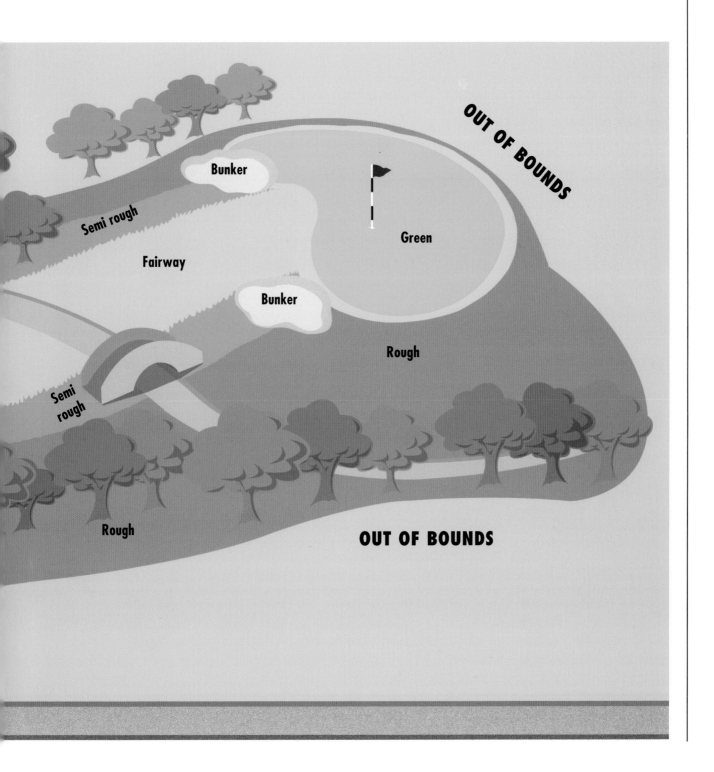

EQUIPMENT – CLUBS

The most important part of a golfer's equipment is their clubs. Each club is designed for a specific type of shot, and will hit the ball to different heights and to different distances. The number of clubs you need can vary, but under the rules you must not have more than 14 clubs in total. Clubs are divided into four main categories: irons, wedges, woods and putters.

IRONS

Irons make up the majority of a set of clubs. They are different lengths and have different amounts of loft.

Each club has a number on it. This makes it easier for the player to know how far it will propel the ball.

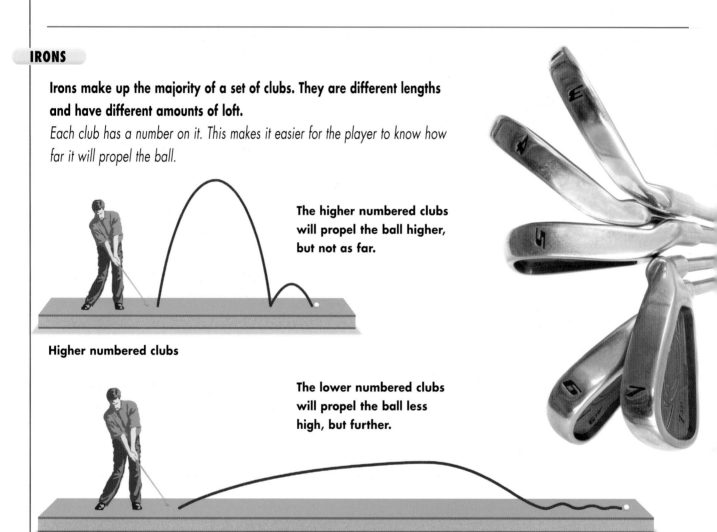

The higher numbered clubs will propel the ball higher, but not as far.

Higher numbered clubs

The lower numbered clubs will propel the ball less high, but further.

Lower numbered clubs

Irons are the most versatile kind of club, and they can be used for various different kinds of shots.

The most common numbered irons are 3, 4, 5, 6, 7, 8 and 9. The 1 to 4 irons are called 'long irons', and keep the ball low in the air. The 5 to 7 irons are called 'mid irons' and give more lift. The irons that loft the ball the highest are the 8 and 9 irons, which are called 'short irons'.

TOP TIP
An easy way to remember how each iron works is that the lower the number on the club, the lower the ball will go.

WEDGES

Wedges look like irons, but are designed for a different purpose. The most commonly used can be recognised because they have letters instead of numbers on them.

P = PITCHING WEDGE
S = SAND WEDGE

Both of these clubs are designed to hit the ball high into the air, so that when it lands on the green it doesn't roll very far.

The sand wedge is shaped so that it glides through the sand. This makes getting out of the bunkers easier. It can also be used to play shots from the grass.

PUTTERS

Putters are the shortest of all the clubs and are designed to roll the ball gently along the ground and not lift it into the air. These clubs are used when the ball is on the green.

Golf clubs are designed for players of average height. Taller or shorter players might need a different length shaft.

WOODS

Woods are the clubs that hit the ball the furthest.

This is due to their length and loft angle. They are called woods because years ago they were actually made from wood!

LOOKING AFTER YOUR CLUBS

Keep your clubs in good condition by cleaning them.

Soak your club heads in warm water and then clean out the grooves with an old toothbrush. Never submerge a wood in water though, just wipe it with a damp cloth. Remember to wipe down the golf grips as well.

OTHER EQUIPMENT

GOLF BALLS

Golf balls come in various colours, but white is by far the most popular.

They tend to have the manufacturer's name on them and a number. The number is purely for identification purposes in case two players are using balls by the same manufacturer.

Optic yellow and orange balls are easier to see, especially in frosty or snowy weather.

GOLF BAGS

These can be either carried using the shoulder straps, or put onto a trolley.

They are used to hold your clubs, spare balls, tees and all your other equipment.

TEES

These small pegs can be made of either wood or plastic, although plastic is more popular.

They are used at the start of each hole on the teeing ground, and hold the ball off the floor, making it easier to hit. They can only be used on the teeing ground.

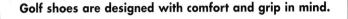

Golf shoes are designed with comfort and grip in mind.

Plastic cleats on the soles of the shoes, which are sometimes called spikes, provide extra traction to reduce the chance of slipping as you swing the club. They also provide more grip when walking on steep or wet slopes.

GLOVE

A glove may be worn to provide extra grip on the handle of the club.

Golf gloves are usually made of leather and are worn on the non-dominant hand. In other words, you would wear them on your left hand if you are right-handed, and on your right hand if you are left-handed.

CLOTHING

Golf is a traditional game and golfers are expected to dress in a certain way.

Shirts should have a collar and trousers or tailored shorts should be worn. Denim jeans and t-shirts without collars are not considered suitable clothing for playing golf. One of the main things to consider when choosing what to wear, is that you need to be comfortable and able to move freely.

An 18-hole golf course can be several kilometres long, so make sure your shoes fit well and are comfortable.

WARMING UP

Flexibility is vital for a good golfing technique, and stretching is the best way to improve this. Good flexibility can also help you create extra power when you swing the club. By performing these simple warm-up exercises you will avoid straining any muscles when you play.

FULL-BODY STRETCH

STEP 1

Start by crouching down low with your feet flat on the floor and your hands in front of you.

STEP 2

Stand up, swinging your arms forwards and up, until you are standing on tiptoe with your arms fully stretched towards the sky.

STEP 3

You should inhale as you stretch up, hold your breath for a moment, then exhale as you bring your arms down and return to a normal standing position.

SHOULDER STRETCH

STEP 1

Hold your right arm out in front of you. Pull it across the front of your body, using the inside of your left elbow to hold it in place.

STEP 2

Hold the stretch for 10 seconds, but be careful not to stretch too far – you don't want to hurt yourself.

STEP 3

Repeat with your left arm.

SIDE STRETCH

LEG STRETCH

Stand back from a wall and place your hands flat against it.
Keeping your right leg straight, bend your left leg at the knee. You should feel the muscles at the back of the right leg being stretched.

Repeat on the other leg.

STEP 1

Place a golf club across the front of your shoulders, keeping it parallel to the ground.

STEP 2

Slowly begin to rotate your shoulders to the right while keeping your hips pointing forwards. When you begin to feel a slight tightness in the side of your body, return to the starting position.

Repeat the stretch by turning in the opposite direction.

The club should remain parallel with the floor throughout this stretch.

The most common golf injuries come from not warming up properly. These include back pain, golfer's elbow (pain on the inside of the upper arm near the elbow) and shoulder pain.

WHAT MAKES THE BALL FLY?

Before you learn how to swing the club, it is important that you understand the correct way to apply the clubhead to the ball to get it to fly.

LIFT AND LOFT

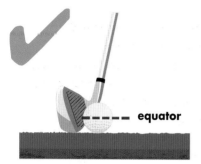

Club face strikes the ball below its equator.

Sole of club hits grass and ball at the same time.

Club face comes through, creating a divot.

Club face strikes the ball too high (e.g. above its equator).

The ball skids along the ground and never lifts off.

This is often called hitting the ball too thin.

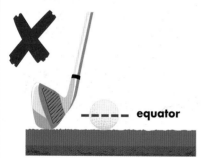

Club face strikes the ground before striking the ball.

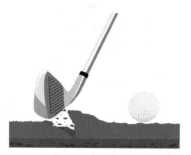

A divot is lifted up but the ball never flies.

This is often called hitting the ball too fat.

THE SWEET SPOT

The ideal point on the clubface to make contact with the ball is known as the sweet spot. This is located in the centre of the clubface. Shots hit from the sweet spot will cause the ball to travel faster and further than shots hit from off-centre.

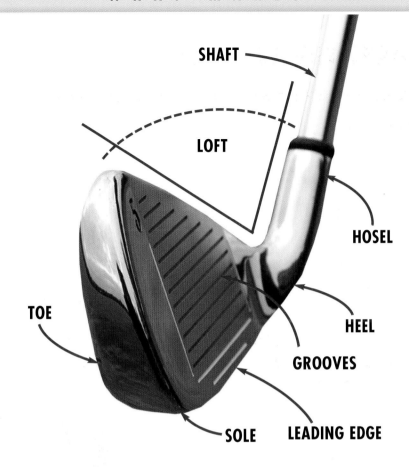

SHAFT

LOFT

HOSEL

TOE

HEEL

GROOVES

SOLE   LEADING EDGE

PARTS OF THE CLUB

SHAFTS

Shafts can be made of steel or graphite.
Graphite shafts can give the ball more distance, but steel shafts are usually more accurate.

Some shafts bend more easily than others – this is called 'flex'.
The most flexible shafts are best for players with slow swing speeds. The stiffest shafts are generally used by players with very fast swing speeds.

CLUBHEADS

Different kinds of clubhead give different amounts of loft.
The grooves on the clubhead make the ball spin in the air – this is called backspin. This helps to carry the ball higher into the air.

CLUB SPEED

The speed at which the clubhead is travelling as it hits the ball will have a big effect on how far the ball travels.

The average club golfer will hit the ball at 80-90 mph (129-145 km/h). Tiger Woods can manage 127 mph (204 km/h). But the fastest hitter in the world is Sean 'The Beast' Fister, who can swing his club at more than 150 mph (241 km/h). Sean was also the World Long Drive Champion in 1995, 2001 and 2005.

Faster speeds = greater distance.
The faster a ball is hit, the further it will travel.

Slower speed = less distance.
A ball that is hit more gently will travel less far.

AIMING THE CLUB

The way you aim the clubface will have a huge effect on the direction in which the ball travels. If you do not aim it correctly, you will not be able to hit your target.

BALL TO TARGET LINE

To aim the club you must:

STEP 1

Firstly, identify a clear target – for example, the flag.

STEP 2

Imagine a straight line that starts at your ball and goes directly towards your target. This is known as the ball-to-target line.

HANDY TIPS

TIP 1

Remember, the ball will go in exactly the same direction as the direction the clubface is pointing. Make sure you aim the club directly at your target.

TIP 2

When you have established your ball-to-target line, look for a target on that line that is close to you – such as a fallen leaf.

This will make it easier to line up the shot accurately.

SQUARE SHOTS

Position the leading edge of the club at a right angle to the ball to target line. This is known as having the clubface 'square' to the ball-to-target line.

CLOSED SHOTS

If you aim the club to the left of the ball-to-target line, this is referred to as 'closed', and this will cause the ball to travel to the left of your target.

OPEN SHOTS

If you aim the club to the right of the ball-to-target line, it is referred to as 'open', and this will cause the ball to travel to the right of your target.

HOLDING THE CLUB CORRECTLY

In the last chapter you discovered how important the clubface is in controlling the direction of the ball. In this chapter you will learn how to hold the club, and the effect it can have on the positioning of the clubface.

GRIP

The correct position for the club (for right-handed golfers) is to have the handle running on a slight diagonal, starting at the middle of the index finger on your left hand and passing across the palm just below the base of the little finger.

STEP 1
As you close your left hand on the club, your thumb should be aligned slightly to the right of centre on the handle.

When you look down you should be able to see two of the knuckles of your left hand.

STEP 2
The top of the handle of the club should extend just over the top of your left hand.

A 'V' shape will be created by your index finger and thumb and this should point between your chin and your right shoulder.

STEP 3
Once the left hand is in place correctly, the right hand can fit into place. The right palm should cover the left thumb and the club should fit comfortably into the first three fingers of the right hand. The thumb and index finger of your right hand will also create a 'V' shape and this should run parallel to the 'V' on the left hand.

TOP TIP
The amount of pressure you apply to the club will have a big impact on how well the club can be swung. Using a scale of one to ten (one being very loose and ten being very tight), your pressure should be four.

STRONG HOLD

If you hold the club with the V pointing too much to your right, this is known as 'too strong'.

Holding the club in this way could cause the club to point left of the target at impact.

WEAK HOLD

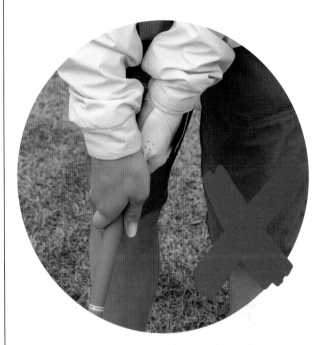

If the V's point is to the left of your chin, it is referred to as 'too weak'.
Holding the club in this way could cause the club to point right of the target at impact.

NEUTRAL HOLD

When you hold the club correctly (as pictured) it is known as a neutral hold. This provides you with the best way of controlling the clubface.

When you begin to play golf, it is tempting to hold the club too tightly. STAY RELAXED and remember the holding pressure should be four.

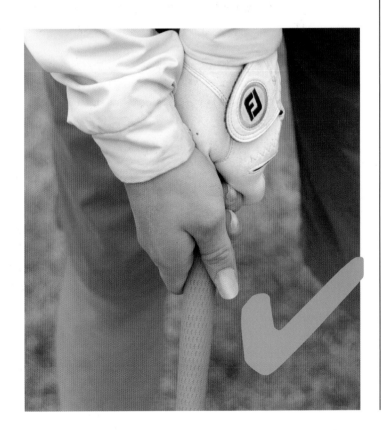

POSTURE – GETTING IT RIGHT

G*ood posture is a very important part of learning to play golf. It influences the way the club travels around your body, the type of contact the club will make with the ground, and your balance during the swing.*

ROUTINE FOR CORRECT POSTURE

If you want to learn how to make successful golf swings, you must first learn how to stand correctly. The best way to achieve the correct posture is by following the routine below:

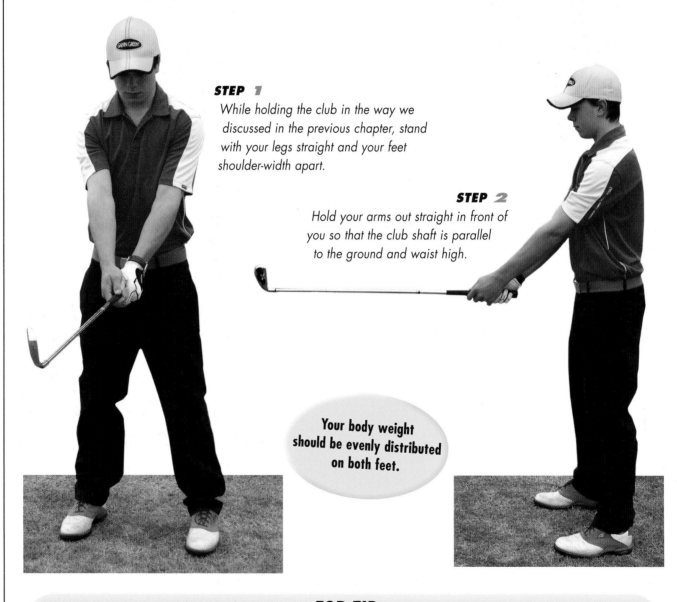

STEP 1

While holding the club in the way we discussed in the previous chapter, stand with your legs straight and your feet shoulder-width apart.

STEP 2

Hold your arms out straight in front of you so that the club shaft is parallel to the ground and waist high.

Your body weight should be evenly distributed on both feet.

TOP TIP

As golf courses are not always flat, you will need to adjust your posture according to the slope. If facing uphill, you should feel more of your weight on your right leg. If facing downhill more of your weight should be on your left leg.

STEP 3

Tilt your upper body forward from the hips, so that the club moves towards the ground. As you do this, you may feel the muscles in the back of your legs tighten – this is perfectly normal.

Feet are shoulder-width apart

STEP 4

Bend your knees slightly – this will take away any tightness felt in the legs and provide you with better stability.

SIMPLE CHECKPOINTS

1) Your arms should feel as though they are hanging from your shoulders, creating a space between your hands and your legs.
2) Your chin should be lifted up and away from your chest, as this will create room for your shoulders to turn.
3) Watching another player from a front-on view, you should notice that their right shoulder is slightly lower than their left shoulder. This is because their right hand is lower than the left hand on the handle of the club.

BODY ALIGNMENT

You have already learnt how to improve your aim by imagining a line from your ball to the target – the ball-to-target line. This line also plays in an important part in helping to align your body correctly.

PARALLEL RAILWAY TRACKS

As you will remember, the clubface must point directly at the target (in other words, it should be square) to the ball-to-target line. You must now get your body parallel to this line. The best way to think about this is by imagining that you are standing on a disused railway track.

STEP 1

Think of the right side of the track as the ball-to-target line, heading straight to your intended target. Your clubface should be aimed in this direction.

STEP 2

The left side of the track is where your feet would be positioned and this should be on a parallel line to the right-hand side of the track.

One great way to practise this technique is to place golf clubs on the ground to help you imagine the tracks.

STEP 3

The easiest way to do this is by starting with your feet together, then carefully moving them to the side one at a time.

Notice that the right shoulder is lower than the left. This is because, for a right-handed player, their right hand is placed below their left. This will be reversed for a left-handed player.

STEP 4

You must also get your knees, hips and shoulders all pointing in the same direction as your feet.

Once you are parallel to the 'train tracks', your body will be aligned correctly.

FULL SWING WITH A WOOD

Wood shots are played when a large amount of distance needs to be covered. Woods are the power clubs, and the most powerful of these is the number 1 wood. This is commonly referred to as a driver. The driver is generally used at the start of each hole on the teeing ground. This means a tee peg can be used to lift the ball off the ground when you are using the driver.

TEEING UP THE BALL

When using the driver, the ball must be put onto a tee.

STEP 1

It is important that the height of the tee is correct. A simple way to position the ball at the correct height is to align the equator of the ball with the top of the driver.

Equator of golf ball

STEP 2

This lifts the ball off the ground enough to allow the club to sweep the ball off the tee without the bottom of the club hitting the ground.

THE SETUP

STEP 1

Position your feet slightly wider than your shoulders, as this will provide better balance with the longer wood club. The ball position should be in line with your left heel, as this will help create a sweeping action with the club.

THE TAKEAWAY

THE BACKSWING

Hands are at
hip height

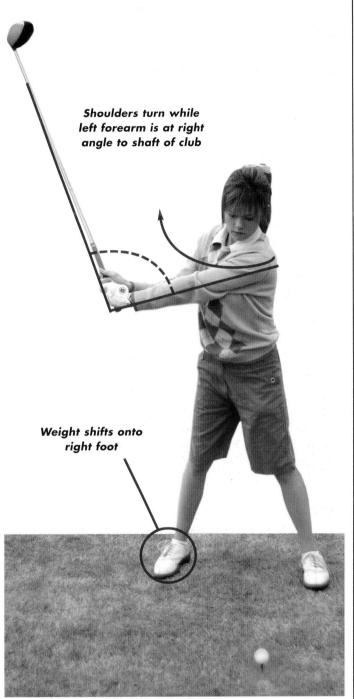

Shoulders turn while
left forearm is at right
angle to shaft of club

Weight shifts onto
right foot

STEP 2
The turn of the shoulders is the movement that starts the takeaway.

As your hands reach hip height, the shaft of the club should be parallel with your feet and the ball-to-target line.

STEP 3
Your shoulders continue to turn, and your body weight should move towards the inside of the right foot.

THE BACKSWING: PART TWO

STEP 4

Hinge your wrists, keeping the right angle between your left forearm and the shaft of the club.

As your upper body turns, your legs should retain their shape and only move slightly. This lower body resistance creates a large portion of the power in the golf swing.

Your left arm should remain straight and your shoulders should be fully turned, with the left shoulder now underneath your chin.

Left arm remains straight

Left shoulder is underneath the chin

Upper body starts to turn

Legs barely move

THE DOWNSWING

STEP 5

The downswing begins with your hips moving towards the target as they begin to unwind.

Move your body weight onto your left foot, and move your shoulders and arms forwards towards the target.

TOP TIP

When taking your club back, your eyes should remain on the ball and your head should hardly move.

THE IMPACT

Head behind ball

Right heel starts to lift off ground

Weight on left side

STEP 6

As the club hits the ball, your hips should have turned beyond their original starting position (the setup).

Your weight should be largely on your left side and your right heel should have begun to lift off the ground. Your head should still be behind the ball at this point, and the clubhead should sweep the ball off the tee without touching the floor.

THE FOLLOW-THROUGH

STEP 7

After the impact, continue to turn your hips and shoulders towards the target.

Move your weight onto your left foot, bringing up your right foot, so that it finishes on its toes. Your knees should finish close together. You will be balancing on your left foot with the club behind your head.

Club finishes behind head

Knees are close together

Right foot finishes on its toes

FULL SWING WITH AN IRON (7 IRON)

Irons are used for shorter shots than woods as you are approaching the green. The number of club you would use depends on the distance that you need to cover. Lower numbered clubs are used from longer distances, and higher numbered clubs are used from closer range.

THE SETUP

Side view

Front view

STEP 1

Make sure the club is aimed correctly at the target, and that good posture and body alignment have been achieved.

You can see from this photo that the ball should be positioned in the middle of your feet. This ball position will help you strike the ball and the ground correctly, and produce the correct amount of spin.

THE TAKEAWAY

The turn of the shoulders is the movement that starts the takeaway.

STEP 2

As your hands reach hip height, the shaft of the club should be parallel with both feet and the ball-to-target line.

STEP 3

As you move your hands above waist height, start to hinge your wrists. By the time the left arm is in a horizontal position, your wrists should be fully hinged.

THE BACKSWING

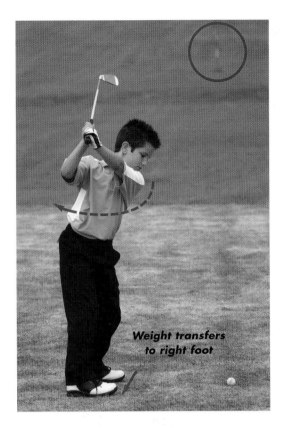

**Weight transfers
to right foot**

STEP 4

**Continue to turn your shoulders, as you move your
body weight towards the inside of your right foot.**

*As your upper body turns, your legs should retain their
position and move only slightly. This lower body resistance
creates most of the power in the golf swing.*

*Keep your left arm straight as you fully turn your shoulders.
Your left shoulder should now be underneath your chin.*

THE DOWNSWING

**Arms and shoulder move
in direction of target**

STEP 5

**The downswing begins with the hips
moving towards the target (the flag)
as they begin to unwind.**

*Move your body weight onto your left foot as
you bring your shoulders and arms forwards
towards the target.*

**Weight transfers
back to left foot**

THE IMPACT

Compare the straight posture of Step 1 (above) to the turned body position in Step 6 (right).

STEP 6

When the club impacts the ball, your hips should have turned beyond their original starting position during the setup.

Your weight should now be largely on your left side, and your right heel should have begun to lift off the ground.

Hips turned towards target

Weight on left side

Heel starts to lift

The sole (bottom) of the club has made contact with the grass and this enables the loft of the club to lift the ball off the ground.

THE FOLLOW-THROUGH

STEP 7

Continue to turn your hips and shoulders towards the target.
Your weight should move totally onto the left foot.
As it does so, lift your right foot up to finish on its toes.

Hips and shoulders move towards target

**Club
finishes
behind
head**

**Knees close
together**

**Right foot finishes
on its toes**

Your knees should finish close
together, and you should be
balancing on your left foot, with
the club behind your head.

Balance is a key ingredient to a
successful golf shot, so swing the
club with a smooth and even tempo.

TOP TIP
Try holding the follow-through position (pictured) until the ball has landed, as this will
improve your balance and help you get used to having most of your weight on one foot.

PITCHING

A pitch shot is generally played from within 100 yards of the green, and the shot can be played with either the pitching or sand wedge. It is the ideal type of shot to play when you are trying to hit the ball over the top of a hazard, such as a bunker or stream. It is also useful if the ground between your ball and the green is uneven, as you will avoid the ball bouncing off-line.

THE SETUP

A good pitch should send the ball high into the air, so that is stops quickly when it lands on the green. It is not a full power shot – the idea is to control the length of your swing to achieve the required shot distance.

STEP 1

Start with your feet slightly narrower than shoulder-width apart.

Hold the club 4 to 5 centimetres further down the handle than you would normally.

STEP 2

Position the ball in the centre of your feet. 60% of your body weight should be on your left foot, and 40% on your right.

THE BACKSWING

STEP 3

Wrists hinge so that the club shaft creates a right angle with the left forearm.

The shorter the backswing length, the less power is generated for the shot.

THE TEMPO

Smooth

STEP 4

Good pitching requires an even tempo throughout the shot. A jerky or uneven action will make it difficult to pitch well.

THE FOLLOW-THROUGH

STEP 5

You should finish with your body weight on your left foot and your upper body facing the target. Your right foot should be slightly raised.

The length of the follow-through should be no shorter than the length of the backswing.

8 o'clock

9 o'clock

10 o'clock

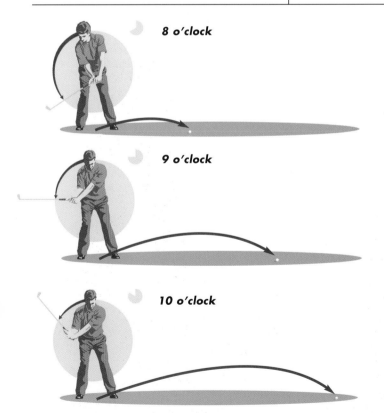

DISTANCE CONTROL

Knowing how far the ball will travel is vital if you are going to play a successful pitch shot. The power and distance that is produced on a shot mainly depends on the length of the backswing made.

Imagine that you are in the centre of a clock face and you have a choice of three different backswing positions: 8 o'clock, 9 o'clock or 10 o'clock. Using your left forearm as the guide, allow your backswing to go to one of these three positions.

You will notice that the shots will travel greater distances as the arm goes back further. With practice and experience you will learn which swing length you require in a particular situation.

TOP TIP
Remember that the later the time you swing to, the further the ball will go.

CHIPPING

A chip shot is used when a player has nearly reached the green, but their ball is not yet on it. The aim is to get the ball as close to the hole as possible. A good chip shot will lift the ball onto the putting green and towards the hole. Power is not a requirement for this part of the game. Therefore, any golfer can master it once they understand some of the key points to the technique.

THE SETUP

Various clubs can be used to play a chip shot, and they will produce various amounts of flight and roll.

STEP 1

Hold the club lower down, so that your right hand is near the bottom of the handle, as this will give you extra control.

Keep your feet close together. 60% of your weight should be on your left side, and 40% on your right.

THE STROKE

STEP 2

Unlike the full shots and pitch shots, you do not hinge the wrists when chipping. Therefore, the club doesn't travel far back and the head of the club should stay below waist height.

The movement should be a pendulum-style action that comes from the shoulders.

The ball should be positioned in line with the inside of your right foot.

CHOOSING THE RIGHT CLUB

Choosing the correct club for the shot you are about to play is a key part of successful chipping. To do this, you must first understand how differently lofted clubs will affect the ball. The diagram below will show you how the ball will react differently when struck with different numbered clubs.

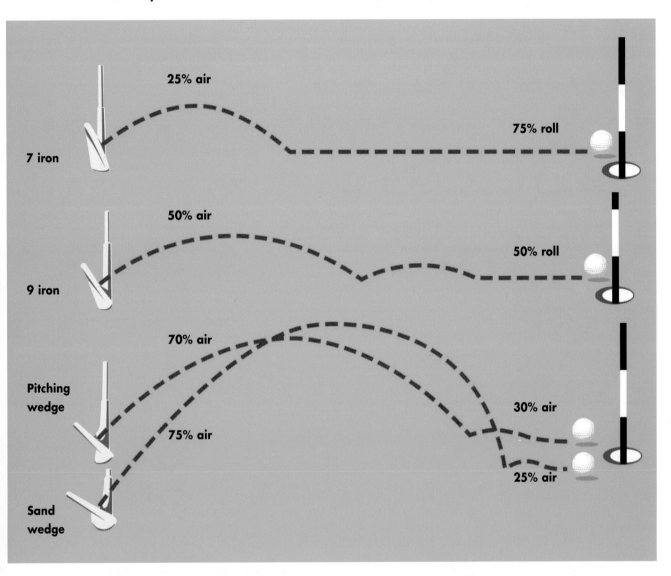

As you can see from the diagram above, the amount of time the ball spends in the air versus the time it spends rolling along the ground depends on which club is being used. Knowing this information is vital if you are to succeed in consistently getting the ball close to the hole.

When you find yourself chipping onto the green, you should ask yourself these two questions:

1 Where exactly do I want the ball to land before it rolls across the green?
2 Where is this chosen point in relation to the current position of the ball and the hole?
Is it, for example, 50% of the way to the hole?

Once you have answered these questions, you can use the information you have learnt in the diagram above to choose the club that is best suited to the task. For example, if the landing point is halfway to the hole, then the club required would be the 9 iron (50% air/50% roll).

BUNKER SHOTS

Bunkers are positioned around the golf course as a type of hazard. They are holes in the ground filled with sand, and a specific technique is required to play them correctly. The most common bunkers you will find are greenside bunkers. They are located in front or to the side of the green, and will catch any shot played towards the green that is slightly off-line. The club used to play from a greenside bunker is the sand wedge.

SPLASH SHOTS

The nickname for a bunker shot is a 'splash shot'. It gets this name because of the way the sand splashes into the air as the shot is played. When this shot is played correctly, the club does not come into contact with the ball at any point. The club hits the sand, and the momentum of the sand as it leaves the bunker lifts the ball out.

THE SETUP

STEP 1

For this type of shot, you want to cut slightly across the ball, so for this reason the body alignment is pointing to the left.

The clubface is fully lofted, but still points in the direction of the flagstick. The hold on the club should only have one knuckle showing – this makes sure the clubface doesn't close (turn left) as it strikes the sand.

The ball position should be five to six centimetres to the left of the centre of the feet.

WHERE YOUR FEET SHOULD BE

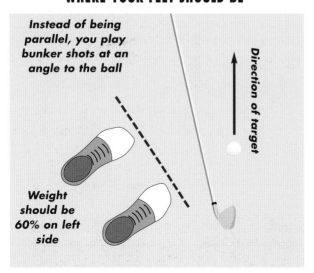

Instead of being parallel, you play bunker shots at an angle to the ball

Direction of target

Weight should be 60% on left side

THE TAKEAWAY

STEP 2

As the shoulders begin to turn, the wrists hinge almost immediately, taking the club on a parallel path to that of the feet and shoulders.

THE BACKSWING

STEP 3

The length of backswing to use depends on the distance the ball needs to travel.

The further the ball needs to go, the longer the backswing must be.

THE DOWNSWING

STEP 4

As the club moves back towards the ball, your eyes should be focused on the sand five to six centimetres behind the ball.

The club should strike the sand five to six centimetres behind the ball. As it does this, it will gather sand and propel the ball out of the bunker.

The positioning of the ball in your stance will allow the ball to be lifted from the bunker with the momentum of the sand.

THE FOLLOW-THROUGH

STEP 5

After playing the shot, your upper body should face the target. The majority of your body's weight finishes on the left side. Your arms should follow through to a length similar to that of the backswing used.

TOP TIP

When you play a bunker shot, the clubhead is not allowed to touch the sand prior to playing a shot, so remember to hover the club above the sand before playing the shot.

PUTTING

The putter is used when the player's ball is on the putting green. The player uses the putter to roll the ball along the green and into the hole – the ball does not lift into the air as it does in other shots. The player must try to get the ball into the hole in as few putts as possible, because each attempt counts as a shot.

THE HOLD

The handle on the putter is a different shape to the other clubs.

It has a flat front, whereas the other clubs have round handles. This is a good reminder that the putter should be held differently.

STEP 1

Place the left hand on the handle, so that the thumb is on the flat part and pointing straight down towards the floor.

STEP 2

Lift the index finger off the handle, ready for the right hand to be placed correctly.

STEP 3

Apply the right hand to the club, making sure that all four fingers of the right hand are placed underneath the raised index finger of your left hand.

STEP 4

Place your thumb onto the flat part of the handle so it points towards the floor.

THE SETUP

STEP 1

Your feet should be shoulder-width apart with the ball slightly to the left of centre.

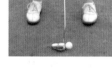

Your body should tilt from the hips, allowing your hands to hang down and under your shoulders.

STEP 2

Knees should be slightly flexed, and your eyes should be directly over the ball.

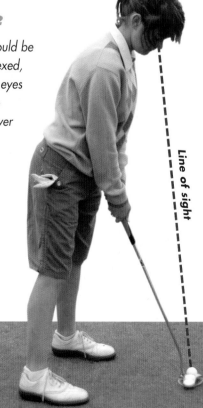

Line of sight

The putter should move in a pendulum-style action that is created by gently rocking the shoulders.

STEP 1

The wrists should not hinge during the putting stroke, but remain straight.

Keep an even tempo throughout the stroke, as this will help develop a better feel for the speed of the greens.

STEP 2

Try to make the length of your backswing and follow-through the same.

READING GREENS

Putting greens are not flat, and it is important that a golfer knows which way the green is sloping, so they can decide where to aim their ball. Working this out is known as 'reading the green', and good golfers are able to judge these slopes and angles very well.

They do this by crouching down behind their ball, and getting low to the ground. From there they are able to see the slope of the green more clearly – from the higher standing position everything looks flat.

The slope will make the ball curve as it rolls along the green – this curve is known as 'break'. A player must use their judgement to estimate the amount of break they think there will be on a putt. They then aim their putter to make up for the curve. For example, if the player thinks the ball will curve 30 centimetres from left to right, they will aim the putter 30 centimetres to the left of the hole, so that the ball will curl round into the hole.

Practice aiming at a small target.
Try aiming at a tee placed into the green. This smaller target will help you improve your aiming skills. It will also make a golf hole look like a really big target in comparison, and this will help your confidence on the greens.

TOP TIP
Try not to leave putts short of the hole. If you always hit the ball hard enough for it to travel as far as the hole, you will quickly become a successful putter.

STAYING SAFE

Safety is an important aspect of golf due to the potential dangers that exist as a result of the speed at which the golf ball can travel, and the speed of the club when it is swung. It is important to be aware of these potential dangers and remember that they can come from other golfers on the course, not just your playing partners.

SHOUTING 'FORE'

When a golf ball is flying through the air, it can be travelling very fast. For example, a professional golfer hitting a ball with a driver will cause the ball to travel at a speed of around 160 mph (257 km/h).

If your shot accidentally travels towards another player, you must warn them that they could be in danger, so that they can protect themselves. You do this by shouting the word 'fore' as loudly as possible. The word 'fore' is believed to have originated in the military as a warning for troops to take cover when something was fired from behind them.

HEARING 'FORE'

If you are playing golf and you hear someone else shout 'fore' you should:

A) *Put your arms up around your head for protection.*

B) *Make yourself as small a target as possible by crouching down. **NEVER** turn to see who shouted 'fore', as a ball could be heading straight at you!*

STANDING IN THE SAFE ZONE

Never stand too close to other golfers when they're taking a shot.

*Remember that a golfer needs plenty of space when they swing a club. The safe zone is behind, facing and slightly to the right of the player. **NEVER** stand directly behind them as you may get hit by their club as they swing.*

FITNESS & DIET

A balanced diet will help you both on and off the golf course. A healthy diet consists of a combination of carbohydrates, proteins and fats, and together they will provide you with the nutrients your body requires.

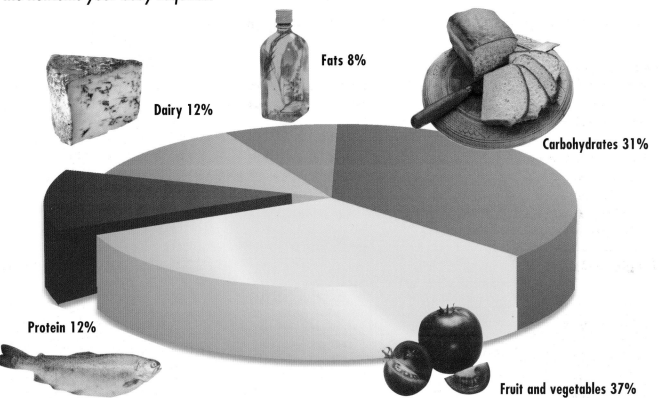

Fats 8%

Dairy 12%

Carbohydrates 31%

Protein 12%

Fruit and vegetables 37%

DIET TIPS FOR GOLFERS

Golf is a game that can take over four hours to play, and it is important that you keep your energy levels up while you play.

Carry fruit, cereal bars and plenty of water in your bag to snack on during your round.
Avoid eating a large meal just before play. A healthy meal eaten two to three hours before the start of the round is ideal. Drink plenty of water during the day and throughout your round.
This will keep you hydrated and will help to make sure your body can perform to the best of its ability.

FITNESS

Flexibility is a key part of being a top golfer. Use the stretching exercises on pages 10-11 to help improve your flexibility.

Golf involves a lot of walking, often with steep hills along the way.
As a golfer becomes tired they find it harder to concentrate and often make mistakes. A good standard of overall fitness will give you a clear advantage.

MENTAL SKILLS

This section is designed to help you with the mental skills required to play golf. A round of golf can take over four hours, so it is important you learn how and when to concentrate.

CONCENTRATION

Firstly, you should understand that you don't need to concentrate for every minute that you are on the course. In fact, to concentrate for such a long time is almost impossible.

You only really need to concentrate when you are about to play a shot, so this will require approximately one minute of concentration per shot. Therefore, if you play 80 shots in a four-hour round, then you need to concentrate for about a quarter of the time.

If you did try to concentrate continuously from the first tee to the 18th green, you would be mentally exhausted long before you finished the round!

CONCENTRATING WHEN IT MATTERS

Concentration is not a resource that we have an endless supply of and must therefore be used sparingly. Think of concentration like an egg timer with the sand inside.

All golfers start with the same amount of concentration, but it is then up to them how they use it.

Players that don't relax between shots will find that all the sand runs out of their egg timer long before the end of their round.

Good players understand that by relaxing between shots they are saving valuable concentration, which will allow them to play all 18 holes without their concentration running out.

By thinking about other things between shots, you will make it easier to blot distracting thoughts out when it comes to taking a shot.

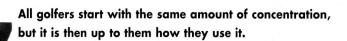

 TOP TIP
One way to relax is to look at wildlife. By counting the different types of animals you see, you can help your brain to recharge, so it is ready for the next shot.

When you hit a bad shot it can be disappointing, but this is not an excuse to sulk.

If you give in to stress and negative feelings, you will play worse as a result. If you expect to mess up a shot, this can become a self-fulfilling prophecy. Try to keep a positive mental attitude. This will help you to concentrate and to play confidently. 90% of winning is in the mind!

To play good golf you must learn how to control your temper. When you hit a bad shot or have some bad luck, getting angry and losing your temper will only make things worse.

All golfers hit poor shots from time to time. But a good golfer quickly forgets about the bad shot, and gets ready to play their next shot.

A golfer that is sulking is easy to spot on the course because their body language is poor.

They tend to walk slowly and without purpose and with their head always looking down to the floor.

Good players walk with a spring in their step and with their heads up and looking straight ahead. They are aware of their surroundings and their actions appear purposeful.

Try to walk with this type of body language between your shots as it will help you arrive at your ball in a better frame of mind.

Remember: champions hit bad shots too, but they react by putting mistakes behind them and moving on.

MICHELLE WIE AND TIGER WOODS

Most people play golf to relax and have fun, but a lucky few get to play professional golf. These players get to travel the world and can be paid huge sums if they are successful.

Tiger Woods was born in Cypress, California on 30 December 1975. He later studied at Stanford University and became a key member of the college golf team. Since he turned pro in 1996, he has taken the golfing world by storm.

He won his first major (The 1997 Masters) at the age of 21, making him the youngest player in history to win the event. He won by 12 shots with a winning score of 18 under-par – an all-time scoring record for the Augusta course.

To date he has won 13 major championships and is on target to beat the record of 18 majors that is held by Jack Nicklaus.

So far he has won prize money of over $74,000,000. When you add to that the money he receives from his sponsors and through advertising, he is one of the richest sportsmen in the world.

Born 11 October 1989, Michelle Wie started playing golf at the age of four in Hawaii. By the time she was eleven, she was regularly winning competitions, often beating her male counterparts.

Growing up, she followed the career of Tiger Woods and this convinced her that she too wanted to be a professional golfer.

At 6 feet tall (180 cm) Michelle can drive the ball over 280 yards (256 m), and her talent at such a young age has helped her become only the fourth female in history to play in a PGA Tour event.

Playing in the Sony Open in January 2004, Michelle missed the halfway cut by only one shot and scored better than 47 men along the way. At the same time she became the youngest player ever to play in a PGA Tour event – she was 14.

In October 2007 Michelle turned 18 and was allowed to join the LPGA (Ladies' Professional Golf Association).

WHERE THE PROS PLAY

ST. ANDREWS, SCOTLAND

Golf has been played at St Andrews, in Scotland, since around 1400 AD, and therefore the Old Course is known throughout the world as the 'Home of Golf'.

What was a simple track hacked through the bushes and heather has developed into six linked golf courses and four other courses in the immediate area, including the Duke's Course, which attract hundreds of thousands of golfing fans from around the world.

AUGUSTA NATIONAL, USA

Augusta National, in Georgia, USA, is home to the first major on the golfing calendar each year – The Masters. It is arguably the most beautiful golf setting in the world.

This picture perfect setting includes the famous Amen Corner, which consists of three holes (the 11th, 12th and 13th). These holes, although beautiful, are also some of the toughest on the course.

PEBBLE BEACH, USA

Pebble Beach is located on the famous 17-Mile Drive in California, USA. This is one of the most stunning coastlines to be found anywhere in the world.

It has been used to host the U.S. Open on several occasions, the most famous one being in 2000, when Tiger Woods won the event by a record-breaking 15 shots.

Jack Nicklaus was famously quoted as saying "If I only had one more round to play, I would choose to play it at Pebble Beach. I loved this course from the first time I saw it. It's possibly the best in the world."

GOLF RULES & ETIQUETTE

There are many rules in golf that cover all types of situations. On these pages you will find some of the basic rules that will help you as you learn to play golf.

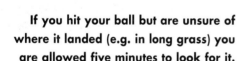

There are some instances during the game where you can pick up the ball and move it – sometimes with a penalty shot and sometimes free.

To drop the ball, you must stand upright, hold the ball at shoulder height and arm's length and simply let go of it. If you drop it and it accidentally touches you, your partner or equipment and rolls closer to the hole, you must drop the ball again.

A penalty shot is one that is added to your score for errors, such as hitting the ball into a water hazard.

If you hit your ball but are unsure of where it landed (e.g. in long grass) you are allowed five minutes to look for it.

If you have not found it after five minutes, it is deemed as lost and you must go back to where you played the previous shot from and drop another ball into play under a penalty.

Grounding the club is when the sole of the club touches the ground prior to playing a stroke. In a bunker or water hazard you are not allowed to ground your club before you hit the ball.

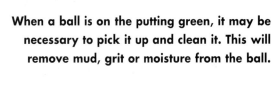

CLEANING THE BALL

When a ball is on the putting green, it may be necessary to pick it up and clean it. This will remove mud, grit or moisture from the ball.

This will help make sure the ball rolls smoothly across the green. Before it can be moved, its position must be marked.

Some courses have ballwashers by the tees. These should be used before teeing off to ensure the ball rolls smoothly.

PLAYING THE BALL AS IT LIES

You are generally not allowed to bend or break anything growing or fixed (e.g. snapping a branch) to improve the position of your ball – except while playing a shot.

You are, however, allowed to remove impediments such as stones, fallen leaves or twigs without penalty, except in a hazard.

PROVISIONAL BALL

If, after playing a shot, you think your ball could be out of bounds or lost, you may play a provisional ball.

You must state it is a provisional ball before it is played. If the original ball is lost you must continue with the provisional ball under penalty of one stroke. If the ball is found you must continue to play with it and the provisional ball must be abandoned.

PENALTY FOR A LOST BALL

If a player's ball is lost or hit out of bounds, they must play another ball under penalty of one shot, as near as possible to the spot from which the original ball was last played.

CASUAL WATER AND ABNORMAL GROUND CONDITIONS

If your ball is in casual water (e.g. a puddle), ground under repair, or a hole made by a burrowing animal (e.g. rabbit), you may drop the ball anywhere within one club length of the start of the obstruction without penalty. However, this must be on the side furthest away from the hole – you cannot move your ball closer to the hole.

HOW TO KEEP SCORE

The number of times that the ball is hit is counted from the first shot on each hole to the final shot when the ball goes in the hole.

SCORE CARD

The score is recorded on a scorecard and when all 18 holes are completed the total score is added together.
If you attempt to hit the ball and miss, it still counts as a shot (this is called an air shot) and must be added to your score.

GOLF HANDICAP

A player's standard can be determined by their handicap. This is a number that tells us on average how many over the total par of the course the player tends to score.

If the total par for a course is 72 and on average the player takes 82 shots, then their handicap would be 10. This system allows players of different skill levels to play against each other, and by subtracting their handicaps you can work out the winner. The maximum handicap is 28 for men and 36 for women.

INFORMATION ON A SCORE CARD

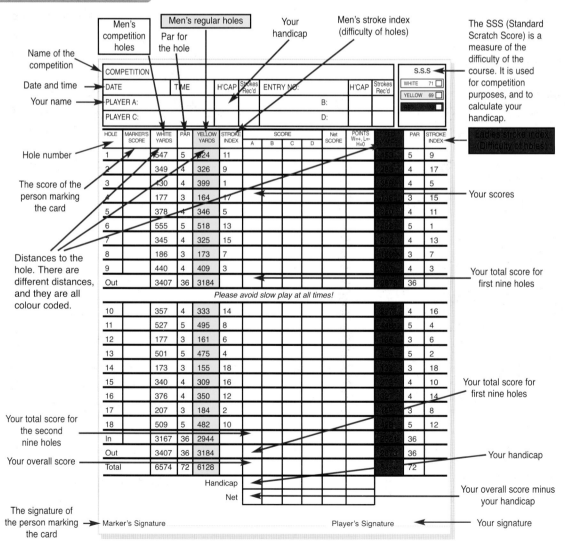

Men's competition holes

Men's regular holes

Your handicap

Men's stroke index (difficulty of holes)

The SSS (Standard Scratch Score) is a measure of the difficulty of the course. It is used for competition purposes, and to calculate your handicap.

Name of the competition

Date and time

Your name

Par for the hole

Hole number

The score of the person marking the card

Distances to the hole. There are different distances, and they are all colour coded.

Ladies stroke index (Difficulty of holes)

Your scores

Your total score for first nine holes

Please avoid slow play at all times!

Your total score for the second nine holes

Your overall score

Your total score for first nine holes

Your handicap

Your overall score minus your handicap

The signature of the person marking the card

Your signature

GOLF IS A QUIET GAME

Never shout, talk loudly or call out to friends. If you are too noisy you could distract other golfers and spoil their fun.

HELP FELLOW GOLFERS

If they are searching for their ball, you may want their help later in the round to look for one of yours.

GOOD SPORTSMANSHIP

Always shake hands with your fellow players at the end of the round. This is a sign of good sportsmanship, which is a key part of golf.

PLAY WITHOUT DELAY

Move off the green as soon as the last player holes out and record the scores on the next tee. This can save a great deal of time over the round.

WATCH YOUR BALL

Keep your eye on the ball until it has stopped, as turning away in a temper can add time to your round in unnecessary searching for the ball.

LET FASTER PLAYERS PLAY THROUGH

If a group is playing faster behind you, let them through. To do this just move to a safe area at the side of the hole and wave the group behind you through.

BEHAVE IN A COURTEOUS MANNER

Club throwing, bad language and cheating are not allowed in golf.

GLOSSARY

AIM *The direction in which the clubface points, affecting the flight direction of the ball.*

BODY ALIGNMENT *The direction in which a player's body faces as they prepare to play a shot.*

BREAK *The curve on the movement of the ball, caused by slopes on the putting green.*

BUNKER *A hole in ground filled with sand, designed as an obstacle.*

CASUAL WATER *A temporary accumulation of water on a course which is not part of a water hazard e.g. a puddle.*

CLUBFACE *The part of the golf club used to make contact with the ball.*

FAIRWAY *The area of short-cut grass that is best for playing shots.*

FLAGSTICK *This is used to indicate the location of the hole on the putting green.*

FORE *A warning used to inform fellow golfers that they may be in danger of being struck by a ball.*

GREEN *A smooth prepared grass area where the flag and hole are located.*

GROUND UNDER REPAIR (GUR) *An area of the course that has been marked out by the maintenance committee for maintenance work to be carried out.*

HOLE *The target of the game, into which the ball must be driven. A hole is also a division of the golf course – there are 18 holes on a course.*

IMPACT *The moment during the swing when the clubface makes contact with the ball.*

IRONS *Irons are individually numbered and make up a majority of any golfer's set of clubs. Each iron will hit the ball a different height and distance.*

LOFT *The angle on the golf club that controls the height of a ball, and the distance it flies.*

LOOSE IMPEDIMENT *Natural objects that include stones, twigs, and branches. These can be moved, providing they are not growing, solidly embedded, or stuck to the ball.*

PAR *Target score of a professional golfer for each hole.*

POSTURE *The position the body is angled at while holding the golf club.*

PUTT *A type of shot played using a specific club (putter) to roll the ball into the hole.*

ROUGH *Long grass that makes playing a shot more difficult.*

TEE *A device designed to raise the ball off the ground. A tee must be no more than 10.16 cm tall.*

TEEING GROUND *The starting point for each hole.*

TEMPO *The speed and rhythm with which the body and club moves.*

WATER HAZARD *Any sea, lake, pond, river or ditch that is defined by the committee with the use of yellow stakes.*

WEDGES *These clubs have the specific purpose of making the ball fly high, so that it stops quickly when landing.*

WOODS *The longest and most powerful clubs in a set, designed to hit the ball long distances.*

LISTINGS

English Golf Union
The National Golf Centre, Woodhall Spa
Lincolnshire, LN10 6PU
Tel: 01526 354500 Fax: 01526 354020
Website: www.englishgolfunion.org

Royal and Ancient Club of St. Andrews
The R&A, St. Andrews
Fife, KY16 9JD
Tel: 01334 460000 Fax: 01334 460001
Website: www.randa.org

USGA (United States Golf Association)
PO Box 708, Far Hills.,
New Jersey, 07931, USA
Tel: 908-234-2300 Fax: 908-234-9687
Website: www.usga.org

International Golf Federation
Golf House, PO Box 708, Far Hills,
New Jersey, 07931-0708, USA
Tel: 908-234-2300 Fax: 908-234-2178
Website: www.internationalgolffederation.org